5/10

	DATE DUE		

Skydiving

Joanne Mattern

ROURKE PUBLISHING

Vero Beach, Florida

www.rourkepublishing.com

PHOTO CREDITS: © vuk8691 : title page; © Drazen Vukelic: page 4; © dzphtovideo: page 5; © Library of Congress: page 6; © Christophe Michot: page 7; © Drazen Vukelic: pages 9, 10; © Marcel Jancovic: page 11; © Drazen Vukelic: pages 12, 13, 14; © Atlaspix: page 15; © Marcel Jancovic: page 16; © Drazen Vukelic: page 19; © Drazen Vukelic : page 20; © Joggie Botma: page 21; © Maksym Dragunov: page 22

Edited by Jeanne Sturm

Cover and Interior designed by Tara Raymo

Library of Congress Cataloging-in-Publication Data

Mattern, Joanne, 1963-
 Skydiving / Joanne Mattern.
    p. cm. -- (Action sports)
 ISBN 978-1-60694-362-5
 1. Skydiving--Juvenile literature. I. Title.
 GV770.M35 2009
 797.5'6--dc22
                                    2009006067

www.rourkepublishing.com – rourke@rourkepublishing.com
Post Office Box 643328 Vero Beach, Florida 32964

TABLE OF CONTENTS

Just Jump!	4
Skydiving's Early Days	6
Equipment	10
Learning to Dive	14
Steering and Turning	16
Skysurfing and Freestyling	18
Team Formations	20
Skydiving Competitions	22
Glossary	23
Index	24

JUMP!

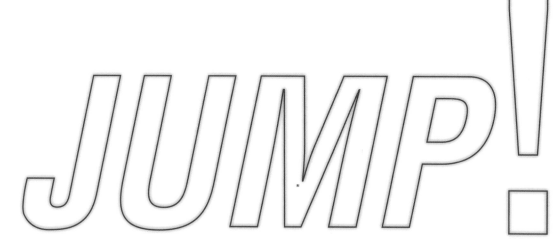

Have you ever dived into a pool? Some people like to dive into the air! **Skydiving** is an **extreme sport**. People who skydive jump out of airplanes. They free-fall to the ground using a **parachute** to slow them down. Skydiving is an exciting sport!

DID YOU KNOW?

Most skydivers jump out of an airplane around 14,000 feet (4,267 meters) above the ground.

Skydiving's Early Days

Skydiving started long before airplanes were invented. People used parachutes to jump from tall buildings hundreds of years ago. In 1797, a Frenchman named Andre-Jacques Garnerin used a parachute to jump out of a hot-air balloon. He jumped about 2,000 feet (610 meters) to the ground.

Platform

The first parachute jump from an airplane was made in 1912. In 1914, Georgia "Tiny" Broadwick became the first woman to jump out of an airplane.

Early skydivers used parachutes attached to the plane. Then they cut the ropes to fall from the plane. In 1919, Leslie Irvin tested a new kind of parachute. This parachute had a **ripcord**. He jumped out of a plane and pulled the ripcord after a few seconds. Many people call Irvin the inventor of skydiving.

DID YOU KNOW?

Until Leslie Irvin did it, people did not think it was possible to jump with a parachute that was not attached to a plane. They thought the skydiver would faint before he or she could pull the ripcord.

Equipment

Skydivers use several different pieces of equipment when they jump. The most important piece is the parachute. Skydivers have two parachutes. One is called the main parachute. The other is the reserve parachute. Skydivers use the reserve parachute if the main parachute does not work.

Skydivers also need an **altimeter**. An altimeter tells skydivers how high they are in the sky. When the skydiver gets to a certain height, it's time to pull the ripcord and release the parachute.

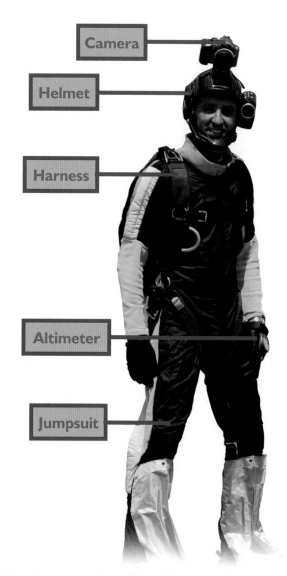

Camera

Helmet

Harness

Altimeter

Jumpsuit

DID YOU KNOW?

Parachutes come in different shapes and sizes, depending on what type of skydiving they are used for.

Skydivers wear **jumpsuits**. These jumpsuits fit tightly. A tight fit helps the skydiver move more quickly through the air. Skydivers wear gloves to keep their hands warm. A **harness** holds the parachutes to the body.

Skydivers also wear helmets and **goggles**. A helmet protects the skydiver's head. It's important to stay safe, both in the air and during landing.

SHIELDS AND GOGGLES

Skydivers wear goggles or helmets that have face shields. Goggles and shields protect the skydiver's face. They also keep wind and dust out of the skydiver's eyes.

Learning to Dive

Skydivers must take training classes before they take to the sky. During these classes, they learn how to use their equipment. They learn all the safety rules.

Next, skydivers do ground training. They jump off of low towers. They learn how to hold and move their bodies in the air. They also learn how to land safely.

Finally, it is time to go up in the air. Usually, a **novice** skydiver will do a **static line jump** or with an instructor. The instructor helps the skydiver do everything right. Later, the skydiver can jump all alone.

DID YOU KNOW?

Some novices start with a static line jump. A metal rope holds the parachute to the airplane. The line opens the parachute when the skydiver jumps.

Steering and Turning

The parachute is not just something to help the skydiver land. It also helps the skydiver fly! A skydiver steers a parachute by pulling on control lines. These lines turn the parachute left or right.

Some skydivers use their parachutes for target practice. They try to land in a certain spot on a field. It takes careful steering and turning to land on the right spot!

In some **competitions**, the landing target is a tiny disc just over one inch (2.54 centimeters) across!

In competition, skydivers earn points for landing on the target.

Skysurfing and Freestyling

Some skydivers have taken this sport to an even more exciting level. These skydivers actually surf in the air. A **skysurfer** attaches a board to his or her feet. The skydiver uses the board to surf in the air, just like a surfer uses a surfboard to ride the waves.

The first standing skysurf was performed by French skydiver Joel Cruciani in 1987. He used a regular surfboard with snowboard foot bindings.

Freestyling is another exciting twist on skydiving. A freestyler performs different **acrobatic** moves during free fall. Freestyle teams have at least two members. One member does the moves. The other member films the skydiver using a helmet-mounted camera.

DID YOU KNOW?

Freestylers can perform a great number of acrobatic moves during their short time in midair.

Team Formations

You can skydive by yourself. However, some people skydive in teams. This sport is called **formation skydiving**. Formation skydiving teams usually jump from a height of 12,500 feet (3,810 meters). Members link hands as they free-fall through the sky. Team members make patterns, such as stars and circles. Finally, the divers let go and pull their ripcords.

Canopy formation is another type of team skydiving. Canopy formation teams open their parachutes right away. Then they link together. Their colorful parachutes look beautiful in the sky.

Formation teams have only 30 to 50 seconds to complete their formations before they have to release their parachutes.

Skydiving Competitions

There are many different skydiving competitions. Many countries hold competitions for skydiving, skysurfing, and freestyling. These events feature many different contests.

There are also **professional** skydiving tours. One tour is called the SkySports International (SSI). Skydivers compete all over the world in SSI competitions. Skydiving is also part of the Summer X Games.

THE MAN BEHIND THE CAMERA

Joe Jennings is a champion freestyler and cameraman. He takes amazing photos while he and his partner freestyle and free-fall through the sky.

GLOSSARY

acrobatic (ak-ruh-BAT-ik): gymnastic acts

altimeter (AL-tuh-mee-tuhr): a device that measures how high in the air you are

canopy (KAN-uh-pee): a wide parachute

competitions (kom-puh-TIH-shuhnz): contests

extreme sport (eks-TREME SPORT): a sport that involves danger and excitement

formation skydiving (for-MAY-shuhn SKY-dy-ving): a type of skydiving where teams make patterns in the sky

free-fall (FREE-fall): to drop through the air without stopping

freestyling (FREE-sty-ling): a type of skydiving where teams film each other doing tricks in the air

goggles (GOG-uhlz): tight, thick glasses that protect a person's eyes

harness (HAR-nuhss): a device that straps a person to something

jumpsuits (JUMP-soots): tight-fitting, one-piece outfits

novice (NAH-vuhss): someone who is new at something

parachute (PA-ruh-shoot): a large piece of fabric attached to thin ropes that lets a person float in the air

professional (pruh-FESH-uh-nuhl): someone who is paid to do something

ripcord (RIP-kord): a string or wire that is pulled to open a parachute

skydiving (SKYE-div-ing): the sport of jumping from an airplane and landing with a parachute

skysurfer (SKYE-sur-fuhr): a skydiver who uses a board to surf through the air

static line jump (STAT-ik LINE JUMP): a type of jump where the skydiver is attached to the plane by a wire

INDEX

altimeter   10
Broadwick, Georgia "Tiny," 8
Cruciani, Joel   18
da Vinci, Leonardo   7
face shields   13
formation skydiving   20
free-fall   4, 20, 22
freestyling   18, 22
Garnerin, Andre-Jacques   6
goggles   12, 13

harness   10, 12
helmet(s)   10, 12, 13, 18
Irvin, Leslie   8
Jennings, Joe   22
parachute(s)   4, 6, 7, 8, 10, 11, 12, 15, 16, 20, 21
ripcord(s)   8, 10, 20
SkySports International   22
skysurfing   18, 22
static line jump   14, 15
X Games   22

WEBSITES TO VISIT

www.dropzone.com
www.joejennings.com
www.uspa.org

ABOUT THE AUTHOR

Joanne Mattern is the author of more than 300 books for children. She has written about a variety of subjects, including sports, history, biography, animals, and science. She loves bringing nonfiction subjects to life for children! Joanne lives in New York State with her husband, four children, and assorted pets.